COOL

Plastic

PROJECTS

Creative Ways to Upcycle Your Trash into Treasure

A Division of ABDO
ABDO
Publishing Company

PAM SCHEUNEMANN

visit us at www.abdopublishing.com

Published by ABDO Publishing Company, a division of ABDO,
P.O. Box 398166, Minneapolis, Minnesota 55439. Copyright
© 2013 by Abdo Consulting Group, Inc. International
copyrights reserved in all countries. No part of this book may
be reproduced in any form without written permission from
the publisher. Checkerboard Library™ is a trademark and
logo of ABDO Publishing Company.

Printed in the United States of America, North Mankato,
Minnesota
062012
092012

 PRINTED ON RECYCLED PAPER

DESIGN AND PRODUCTION: ANDERS HANSON, MIGHTY MEDIA, INC.
SERIES EDITOR: LIZ SALZMANN
PHOTO CREDITS: SHUTTERSTOCK

The following manufacturers/names appearing in this book
are trademarks: Americana® Multi-Purpose™ Sealer, Artist's
Loft™, Arrow®, Fiskars®, Glitter Glue™, Mod Podge®,
Sharpie®, Singer®, Westcott™

LIBRARY OF CONGRESS CATALOGING-IN-PUBLICATION DATA

Scheunemann, Pam, 1955-
  Cool plastic projects : creative ways to upcycle your trash
into treasure / Pam Scheunemann.
      pages cm -- (Cool trash to treasure)
  Includes index.
  ISBN 978-1-61783-437-0
  1. Plastics craft--Juvenile literature. 2. Salvage (Waste, etc.)-
-Juvenile literature. I. Title.
  TT297.S2985 2012
  745.572--dc23
                              2012000685

TABLE of CONTENTS

TRASH
TO Treasure

The days of throwing everything in the trash are long over. Recycling has become a part of everyday life. To recycle means to use something again or to find a new use for it. By creating treasures out of trash, we are also *upcycling*. This is a term used to **describe** making useful items out of things that may have been thrown away.

It is very important to look for ways to reuse and upcycle plastic. Only a small part of the plastic we use can be recycled. Many plastic items are marked with a number inside a triangle. This number shows what type of plastic it is made of. It does not mean it is recyclable.

Permission and Safety

- Always get **permission** before making any type of craft at home.
- Ask if you can use the tools and materials needed.
- Ask for help when you need it.
- Be careful when using knives, scissors, or other sharp objects.
- Have an adult help you handle hot items.

Be Prepared

- Read the entire activity before you begin.
- Make sure you have everything you need to do the project.
- Keep your work area clean and organized.
- Follow the directions carefully.
- Clean up after you are finished for the day.

Plastic is made from many different **chemicals**. Not all of the chemicals can be mixed or reused to make more plastic. For example, drink bottles can be recycled. But the caps are made from a different kind of plastic. If they were mixed together, it would ruin the new plastic. So take a fresh look at the plastics around your home. Could they be upcycled into something new? See what you can come up with. The sky's the limit.

In this book you'll find great ideas to upcycle different kinds of plastic. Make them just like they appear here or use your own ideas. You can make them for yourself or as gifts for others. These projects use easy-to-find tools and materials.

PLASTIC

Many everyday items are made out of plastic. Plastic can be found all around us. And recycling is not an **option** for many types of plastic. Here are some ideas for reusing or upcycling plastic.

Plastic Bottles

- FLOWER POTS
- VASES
- PIGGY BANK OR CHANGE JAR

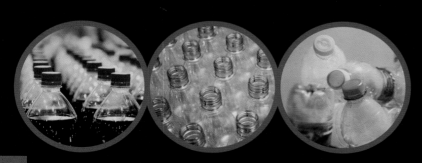

Bread Bag Tags

- LABELS FOR ELECTRIC CORDS, SPARE KEYS, AND GARDEN PLANTS
- USE ONE TO MARK THE END OF A ROLL OF TAPE

Gift Cards & Credit Cards

- CABLE/CORD ORGANIZER
- JEWELRY
- COASTERS
- GUITAR PICKS

Mesh Produce Bags

- SOAP HOLDER
- POT SCRUBBER
- VEGETABLE SCRUBBER
- REUSEABLE PRODUCE BAG
- BAG FOR CONTAINER LIDS

CD Jewel Cases

- PICTURE FRAMES
- DISPLAY FOR A BUTTERFLY COLLECTION
- DESKTOP CALENDAR STAND
- COASTERS

Plastic Buttons

- MAGNETS
- JEWELRY
- GREETING CARD DECORATIONS

TOOLS & MATERIALS

1/8-INCH (3 MM) HEAVY DUTY HOLE PUNCH

1/2-INCH (1 CM) MAGNETS

10 MM JUMP RINGS

ACRYLIC PAINT

ALL PURPOSE SEALER

CARD STOCK

CHAIN NECKLACE

CHALK

CHALKBOARD PAINT

CRAFT FELT

DECORATIVE GEMS

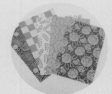

DECORATIVE PAPER

FLAT-NOSED PLIERS

FLORAL STEM WIRE

GLITTER GLUE

GREEN CHENILLE STEMS

HOT GLUE & GLUE GUN

JEWEL CASE

JOURNAL

MOD PODGE

NEEDLE-NOSED PLIERS

OLD COMPUTER
KEYBOARD KEYS

OLD GIFT CARDS

PAINT PENS

PLASTIC BOTTLE TOPS

PLASTIC BREAD BAG
TAGS

PLASTIC BUTTONS
WITH HOLES

PLASTIC MESH
PRODUCE BAG

PLASTIC TUB LID

SQUARE ARTIST'S
CANVAS

STAR-SHAPED HOLE
PUNCH

TOGGLE CLASP

- **PLASTIC BUTTONS WITH HOLES**

- **MARKER**

- **PAPER**

- **SCISSORS**

- **CRAFT FELT**

- **TAPE**

- **FLORAL STEM WIRE**

- **GREEN CHENILLE STEMS**

- **GLITTER GLUE**

- **DECORATIVE GEMS**

- **VASE**

BUTTON BOUQUET

A great way to reuse buttons!

1. Make **stacks** of two or three buttons that look good together.

2. Draw circles and flower shapes on a piece of paper. Make them different sizes. Cut them out.

3. Select colors of felt that go with the buttons. Roll up a piece of tape and put it on a paper shape. Stick it to the felt. Cut around the paper shape. Use the paper shapes to cut out more felt shapes.

Continued on the next page

11

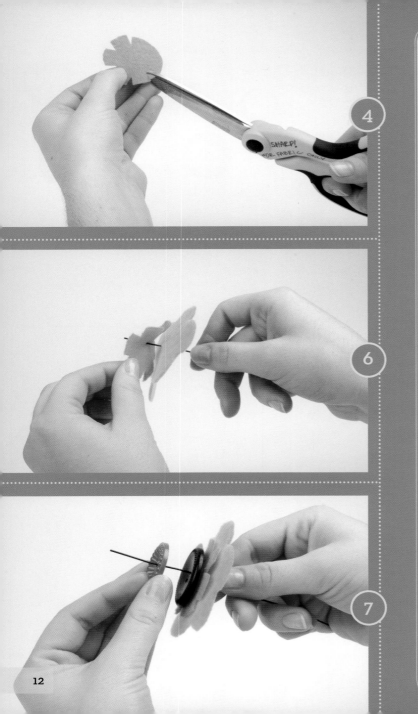

4 You can cut little triangles into the felt circles to make flowers.

5 Try different **combinations** of felt and buttons. **Stack** the buttons on top of the felt shapes. Rearrange them until you like the way it looks.

6 Choose one stack to start with. Poke a piece of floral stem wire through the center of the bottom felt shape. Then poke it through the center of any other felt shapes in the stack.

7 Stick the wire through the holes in the buttons.

8   Bend the wire and push it back through the buttons. Use different holes in the buttons.

9   Push the buttons up to the bend in the wire. Poke the wire back through the felt. Pull tight so the buttons are against the felt. Twist the ends of the wire together to make one stem.

10   Twist the end of the chenille stem around the wire just under the felt. Wrap the chenille stem around the wire stem.

11   Decorate the felt with glitter glue and decorative gems.

12   Repeat steps 6 through 11 to make more button flowers. Put them in a vase!

STUFF YOU'LL NEED

- **HEAVY CARD STOCK**
- **RULER**
- **MARKER**
- **SCISSORS**
- **USED GIFT CARDS**
- **1/8-INCH HEAVY-DUTY HOLE PUNCH**
- **10 MM JUMP RINGS**
- **FLAT-NOSED PLIERS**
- **TOGGLE CLASP**

A CREDIT TO YOUR WRIST

Charge ahead with this bracelet!

1 Draw a ³/₄-inch (2 cm) square on card stock and cut it out. Cut a tiny bit off each corner. This is the bead **template**.

2 Place the template on a gift card. Pick a spot that has a cool pattern or words. Trace around it with the marker. Cut it out. This is one of the beads for your bracelet.

3 Repeat step 2 to make more beads. You will probably need between five and seven beads for a bracelet.

4 Mark four dots on the template. They should be in the same place in each corner. Use the hole punch to punch a hole over each dot. Make sure the holes aren't too close to the edge of the card stock.

Continued on the next page

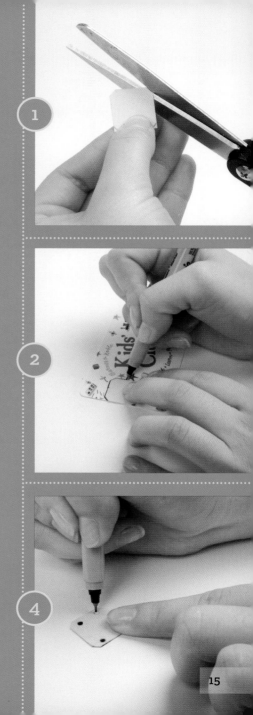

15

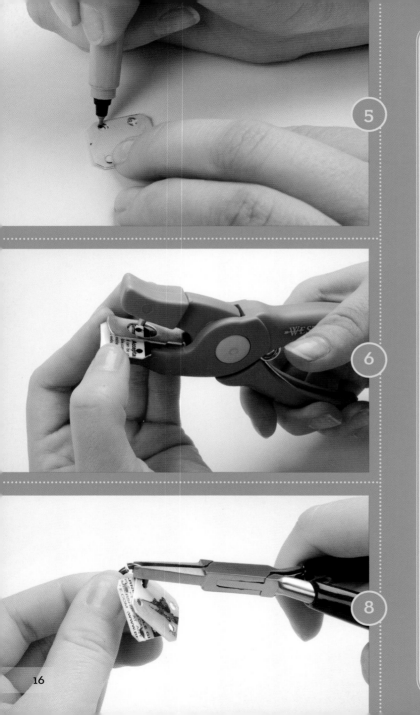

5 Turn a bead face down. Put the **template** on a bead. Position the template with the holes toward the sides of the bead. Fill in the holes with the marker.

6 Use the hole punch to punch out all the holes in the bead.

7 Repeat steps 5 and 6 for all the beads.

8 Line the beads up in the order you want them to be in the bracelet. Start at one end. Put a jump ring through one of the top holes in the end bead. Then put it through the top hole in the next bead. Hold one side of the jump ring with the flat-nosed pliers. Twist the ring so the ends line up.

9 Keep using jump rings to add beads. Hold it around your wrist to test the length. Stop adding beads when there is about 1 inch (2.5 cm) between the ends.

10 Put jump rings through the top and bottom holes in the last bead. Close the jump rings. Put both of them through a third jump ring. Do the same with the first bead.

11 Attach one half of the clasp to the third jump ring on each end.

17

STUFF YOU'LL NEED

- **PLASTIC BAG TAGS**

- **1/8-INCH HEAVY-DUTY HOLE PUNCH**

- **ACRYLIC PAINT**

- **PAINTBRUSH**

- **PAINT PENS**

- **ALL PURPOSE SEALER**

- **DECORATIVE GEMS**

- **GLUE**

- **JUMP RINGS**

- **CHAIN NECKLACE**

- **FLAT-NOSED PLIERS**

- **TOGGLE CLASP**

Bag Tag Necklace

You'll look fresh in this beauty!

1. Punch a hole in one corner of 14 small bag tags. Put the hole in the same spot on all the tags. Punch two holes in the top of a large bag tag.

2. Paint one side of the tags white. Let the paint dry. Then paint the other side. Let the paint dry. Then paint each tag with a background color. Do one side and then the other. Let the paint dry between sides. It will take a few coats of paint to cover the tags well.

3. Use paint pens to decorate the tags. Don't forget to do both sides. Let the paint dry between sides. Put a coat of all-purpose sealer on both sides of each bead. Let it dry. Then glue on some decorative gems. Let the glue dry.

4. Put a jump ring through the hole in a tag. Then put it through a link in the chain. Hold one side of the jump ring with the flat-nosed pliers. Twist the ring so the ends line up. Attach all of the small tags to the chain this way. Attach the large tag in the middle using two jump rings. Arrange the tags any way you want!

5. Decide how long you want the **necklace** to be. Use the pliers to remove any extra links from the chain. Add a toggle clasp to join the ends together.

19

- CD JEWEL CASE
- CARD STOCK
- RULER
- SCISSORS
- GLUE
- PHOTO OR ARTWORK
- RIBBON
- DECORATIVE PAPER
- DECORATIVE GEMS

ALL STAR

JEWEL CASE FRAME

A good case for upcycling!

1. Open the CD case. Snap out the tray that holds the CD. Remove all paper and labels from the jewel case. Wash and dry it.

2. Cut a square piece of card stock that is 4 3/4 inches (12 cm) on each side.

3. Glue the photo or artwork to the card stock. Decorate the card stock around the picture. You could glue on colorful paper, ribbon, or gems. Or think of your own ideas. Just make sure that the decorations don't stick out past the sides of the card stock.

4. Gently remove the lid of the jewel case. Flip the bottom of the case over. Reattach the lid. The lid should be propped up by the bottom.

5. Slip the card stock behind the tabs in the lid of the CD case. Make sure the picture is against the plastic so it faces out. If you like, you can add decorations to the outside of the frame too!

STUFF YOU'LL NEED

- PLASTIC MESH PRODUCE BAG

- SCISSORS

- 36-INCH (91 CM) RIBBON

- SAFETY PIN

- PLASTIC TUB LID

- CRAFT KNIFE

- RULER

Bag for the Beach

Sand won't mesh with this bag!

1. Cut the top of the mesh bag evenly. Fold the top in about 1 inch (2.5 cm).

2. Pin the safety pin to the end of the ribbon. Weave it in and out of the folded mesh. Keep it about 1/4 inch (.6 cm) from the fold. Go around the entire opening of the bag.

3. Stretch the bag open as wide as you can. Tie the ends of the ribbon together.

4. Have an adult help you use a craft knife to cut a small X in the center of the plastic lid. Put the lid inside the bag.

5. Push a little bit of the bottom of the bag through the X. If there is a metal tab on the bag, push it through the X. It will keep the bag from falling back out. If there is no metal tab, tie a knot in the part of the bag you pushed through the X.

23

Keyboard
Journal
(page 27)

Keyboard
Calendar
(pages
25–26)

STUFF YOU'LL NEED

- **OLD COMPUTER KEYBOARD**
- **FLAT-HEAD SCREWDRIVER**
- **NEEDLE-NOSED PLIERS**
- **SMALL PAINTBRUSH**
- **CHALKBOARD PAINT**
- **ACRYLIC PAINT**
- **COMPUTER & PRINTER**
- **COLORED PAPER**
- **STAR-SHAPED HOLE PUNCH**
- **MOD PODGE**
- **HOT GLUE & GLUE GUN**
- **1/2-INCH (1 CM) MAGNETS**
- **CHALK**
- **CARDBOARD**
- **JOURNAL WITH A PLAIN COVER**
- **RULER**
- **PENCIL**

keyboard calendar

Let these bright keys count the days!

1. Use a flat-head screwdriver to **pry** the keys out of the keyboard. You will need 31 keys the same size plus the space bar.

2. Wash the keys with soap and water. If there is anything sticking out of the backs of the keys, pull it off with a pliers. Make sure the back of each key is flat.

3. Paint the space bar with chalkboard paint. Let it dry.

4. Paint the tops and sides of the other keys with acrylic paint. It will take a few coats of paint. Let the paint dry between each coat.

5. Type the numbers 1 through 31 on your computer. Space them out on the page in rows and columns. Print out the page on colored paper. Cut out each column of numbers. Cut the columns wide enough that the star hole punch can fit over the numbers.

Continued on the next page

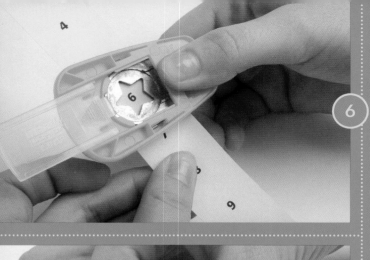

6 Center the star-shaped hole punch over each number. Punch out the numbers.

7 Paint the top of a key with Mod Podge. Gently press a star number on top. If it sticks over the edge, just press the edges down. Put a coat of Mod Podge over the whole key. Glue the other 30 star numbers to keys the same way. Let the Mod Podge dry completely.

8 Have an adult help you use the hot glue gun. Glue a magnet to the back of each key. Try to keep the magnets even with the backs of the keys. Glue two magnets to the back of the space bar. Let the glue dry completely.

9 Put the magnets on the refrigerator or other metal surface. Write the current month on the space bar with chalk. Arrange the days of the month underneath it.

KEYBOARD JOURNAL

The cover is key!

1 Use a flat-head screwdriver to **pry** the keys out of the keyboard. Wash the keys with soap and water. If there is anything sticking out of the backs of the keys, pull it off with a pliers. Make sure the back of each key is flat.

2 On a piece of cardboard, arrange the keys the way you want them to go on the journal cover. Make sure the arrangement is smaller than the journal.

3 Measure the size of your arrangement. Mark an area that size on the journal cover in pencil.

4 Have an adult help you use the hot glue gun to glue the keys to the journal cover. Start in one corner. Make a square of glue the same size as a key. Press the key into the glue. Position it quickly before the glue hardens. Glue on the rest of the keys one at a time. Let the glue dry completely.

27

- SQUARE ARTIST'S CANVAS
- RULER
- PENCIL
- ACRYLIC PAINT
- PAINTBRUSH
- MARKER
- PLASTIC BOTTLE TOPS
- DECORATIONS
- GLUE
- GLITTER GLUE

BOTTLE TOP POP ART

Take your art to the top!

1. Use a ruler and pencil to divide the **canvas** into squares. Make sure each square is at least as big as a bottle top.

2. Paint each of the squares a different color. When the paint is dry, use a fat marker to outline the squares.

3. **Decorate** the insides of the bottle tops. Glue on gems, buttons, foam, or whatever you like. Use your creativity and a lot of glitter glue!

4. Glue each bottle top inside one of the squares. Let the glue dry.

29

CONCLUSION

Now you know what upcycling is all about. What hidden gems do you have around your house? Do you have relatives who need their **attic** cleaned? What about **garage** and yard sales? Are there **thrift stores** and reuse centers near you? These are all great sources for materials that you can upcycle!

There are many benefits to upcycling. You can make some really great stuff for yourself or gifts for your family and friends. You can save useful things from going into the trash. And the best part is, you don't have to spend a lot of money doing it!

So keep your eyes and ears open for new ideas. There are many Web sites that are all about recycling and upcycling. You might find ideas on TV or in magazines. There are endless ways that you can make something beautiful and useful from **discarded** materials. Remember, the sky's the limit!

GLOSSARY

ATTIC – a room right under the roof of a building.

CANVAS – a piece of cloth that is stretched over a frame and used as a surface for a painting.

COMBINATION – two or more things put together in a certain way.

DESCRIBE – to tell about something with words or pictures.

DISCARD – to throw away.

PRY – to separate two things by sticking something between them and pushing them apart.

GARAGE – a room or building that cars are kept in. A *garage sale* is a sale that takes place in a garage.

NECKLACE – a decoration that is worn around the neck.

OPTION – something you can choose.

PERMISSION – when a person in charge says it's okay to do something.

STACK – a pile of things placed one on top of the other.

TEMPLATE – a shape you draw or cut around to copy it onto something else.

THRIFT STORE – a store that sells used items, especially one that is run by a charity.

Web sites

To learn more about cool craft projects, visit ABDO Publishing Company on the World Wide Web at www.abdopublishing.com. Web sites about creative ways for upcycling trash are featured on our Book Links page. These links are routinely monitored and updated to provide the most current information available.

INDEX

My **k** Book

Book

by Jane Belk Moncure
illustrated by Linda Hohag

THE CHILD'S WORLD

ELGIN, ILLINOIS 60120

1990 EDITION

Library of Congress Cataloging in Publication Data

Moncure, Jane Belk.
  My "k" book.

  (My first steps to reading)
  Rev. ed. of: My k sound box. © 1979.
  Summary: Little k goes for a walk dressed up like a
king and finds many items beginning with "k" to put in
his box.
  1. Children's stories, American.   [1. Alphabet]
I. Hohag, Linda. ill.   II. Moncure, Jane Belk.   My k
sound box.   III. Title.   IV. Series: Moncure, Jane Belk.
My first steps to reading.
PZ7.M739Myk   1984   [E]   84-17539
ISBN 0-89565-284-6

Distributed by Childrens Press, 5440 North Cumberland Avenue,
Chicago, Illinois 60656

My "k" Book

Little  k had a box.

He said, "I will fill my  box.

"But first I will be a king."

He dressed up like a king.

Little  went for a walk.

He found a koala.

Guess where he put
the koala?

box

Little  found

kingbirds.

Guess where
he put the
kingbirds?

Then he found

a kitten.

"Kitty, kitty," he called.

Lots of kittens came...

lots and lots of kittens.

Little  said, "I will put you into my box."

But the kingbirds said,
"No! No! No!"

So, Little  k found a ...

kangaroo.

The kangaroo had a pocket.

Little **k** put the kittens into the kangaroo's pocket.

"A king can do anything!" said Little .

So he played a kettledrum.

Then he put it into his box.

Then he found a 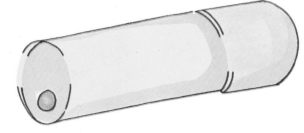 kaleidoscope.

He looked in the little hole.
This is what he saw.

Then he found kites, kites, kites.

"I will fly a kite," he said.

But the kite flew away.
The kingbirds flew away.

The kittens kicked the kangaroo.
The kangaroo

sneezed, "Kerchoo!" and blew...

all of them into a ...

kindergarten,

surprising the kids.

25

kites

koala

kingbird

kittens

kettledrum

kitten

What fun they had!

kangaroo

kaleidoscope

kingbird

kitten

kitten

27

More words with Little

kiss

keg

katydid

ketchup

kettle

key

kitchen

kid

kid

kimono

kayak

29